Culinary Kisses presents …

From the Catwalk to the Kitchen

A Collection of Healthy Southern Recipes

By Chef Angela-Michelle

DEDICATION

To my Grandmother, Joannie (Roberts) Lewis

Your love fills my heart, your strength empowers my determination, and
your tenacity fuels my courage. You reside in my memories of the past just
as much as my thoughts in the present. I miss you more and more each day.
I love you, Grandma!

I JOHN 1:9

CONTENTS

ACKNOWLEDGMENTS

There were a number of people who had a hand in cultivating my culinary foundation. It all started with my parents. They met in the kitchen of the restaurant they worked in. My mom was a line cook and my dad was the chef. So now I proudly proclaim myself as the product of a culinary creation.

My culinary expertise was further expanded by my mother's mother, Joannie, and my mother's sisters. They taught me so much. I instinctually learned how to create the perfectly balanced dish without measuring a thing or following any written rules for cooking.

I've been blessed with a gift ... one that I don't take lightly. I thank God for my culinary past, present, and future. I thank God for my family. I thank God for giving me the courage and wisdom to share my recipes with the world.

Photographers: Jessica York, Keith Strickland, and Angela Jordan

1 MY FAMILY HISTORY

To this day it still baffles me how my Great Grandfather, Cisro Roberts (my mother's grandfather) owned a store and several acers of land in Mississippi in the 1800's. My Grandmother, Joannie Roberts, was born in November of 1903. At the age of 18 she married Reed Lewis and inherited her father's store and land. She went on to give birth to 14 children. My mother, Ethel Lewis, was the fourth to the last child.

They lived on the land, farmed it, and feed the neighborhood with the fruits of their labors. Every morning before school my mother had to start a fire in the fire place, milk the cows, pick cotton, cook breakfast, and get ready to meet the school bus by 9:00 a.m. After school she had to pick several more pounds of cotton, clean up, and do her homework, all before going to bed at 9:00 p.m.

Growing up on a farm instilled a stern work ethic and many old school values in my mother and all of her siblings; most of which were handed down to the next generation. There were many life lessons in planting, growing, picking, and selling vegetables. They also had to wash clothes on a washboard, chop wood, drop fertilizer, and grind meat to make and smoke their own sausage. This lifestyle was a tradition of life for my family in Tylertown, Mississippi.

My mom moved to Flint, Michigan when she turned 18 years old. She took a couple of classes at the local college and worked in a restaurant on the south side of town. This is where she met my dad. She eventually abandoned the cook's life and started working at AC Spark Plugs (as it was known back then). Flint was the place to be in the 60's and 70's with the big three in the automotive industry thriving on automotive manufacturing sales.

It didn't matter if my mother was working in a restaurant or an automotive plant, she was always cooking and baking at home. Smothered chicken, fried okra, rice and gravy, collard greens, cornbread, macaroni and cheese, green beans, candied yams, and egg custard pie were nothing for her to whip up on a moment's notice. No matter what my mother was cooking or baking, she always had me in the kitchen with her. When I was a toddler, she sat me on the kitchen counter as she creamed her butter and sugar together to make her infamous German chocolate cake. I would dip my fingers in the bowl when she turned her back to grab a taste of the butter-sugar mixture. To this day I truly don't know why that particular concoction was so delicious to me … but it was. Regardless, the development of my culinary foundation was off to a great start.

My mama knew her stuff, but she learned from one of the best … her mother. My Grandfather passed away from cancer 4 years before I was born. A few years after that, my Grandmother left her farmhouse in Mississippi and joined her children in Michigan. She eventually settled in a small rural town known as Chesning, which is about 40 minutes north of Flint. We're talking dirt roads, no sidewalks, and vast farm lands as far as I could see. One of my aunts and her husband built a house next door to my Grandmother. I spent a lot of time there: weekends, holidays, and summers. It was my home away from home. It was during this time in my life I learned how to plant, grow, and harvest vegetables (on a much larger scale from the garden my mom and I had in our back yard), how to wring a chicken's neck and pluck its feathers, and how to chase a cow down and get it back into the barn when it broke free in the middle of the night.

I didn't know it at the time, but this experience played a significant part in the development of my culinary foundation. In addition to the farm life, my Grandmother and my aunts taught me how to cook everything from pineapple upside down cake to homemade dinner rolls to chicken and dumplings. These were strong, black women from the South. They didn't measure the ingredients, they didn't follow any cooking rules, and they surely didn't use a thermometer. Everything they did was purely instinctual. Coupled with the culinary genius genes I inherited from my dad, this background was the best mixture of culinary knowledge I could have. It's priceless.

As I grew older, the more I discovered and explored with food. Even though I spent 25 years on the runway in the fashion industry, I never stopped creating dishes that made me (and others) happy. Many people were in my ear … write a cookbook, open a restaurant … but I was a model and I was loving it. It just wasn't the right time.

Now fast forward a quarter of a century. I was getting older and decided to retire from modeling; even though the people in the industry tried to convince me to stay. I not only inherited my family's instinctual take on food, but I also inherited the fountain of youth from them as well. Just like my mother, and my mother's mother, I do not look my age. Couple that with my natural zest for life and fitness, I could have extended my modeling career another decade … easily. But I somehow knew in my spirit it was time to move on. Things quieted down. I became still. I prayed, and then listened. Soon I heard the call, the call to cook. The time has come.

2 HOLIDAYS AT GRANDMA'S HOUSE

All of my Grandmother's children, both sons and daughters, know how to cook. I mean "really" cook. So you can imagine how the holidays were for our family. Everyone would gather at my grandma's house and cook like tomorrow would never come. It was like a well machined instrument. One of my aunts would snap the beans. When another aunt arrived, she would grab the corn and start cutting it off the cob. Another aunt would make the corn bread and another would season and fry the chicken. It was like the scene in the movie "*Soul Food.*" Dinner at Big Mamma's house in Sunday's after church was a family tradition. It was the same with us, but because my Grandmother lived a little ways away from the city, we held our family gatherings on holidays. The many moving family pieces produced a meal that the finest kings and queens would have enjoyed. And we did!

While my mom and her sisters were in the kitchen cooking, my uncles would be outside cooking. They'd prepare everything from deer to rabbit to raccoons to goat to fish. As a kid I learned how to catch, clean, and fry fish. I also learned how to skin, clean, and cook rabbit with gravy. I even learned how to grind meat and stuff castings to make sausage. But make no mistake, my uncles could and did cook everything my mom and aunts cooked in the kitchen. My Grandmother taught her sons how to cook just as she did her daughters. And they all had that intuitive gift, that natural internal culinary knowledge. That is our family's legacy.

It was these invaluable experiences, coupled with my younger years on the kitchen counter helping my mamma cook, that underconsciously taught me how to cook. I learned how to do it all, from scratch, and without any tools of measurement or time-keeping. Now I have the privilege and honor of sharing some of my family's traditional dishes that I have revamped to reflect a healthier take without sacrificing the nostalgic flavor. I hope you enjoy them with your family and friends for many years to come.

CULINARY KISSES PRESENTS …

FROM THE CATWALK TO THE KITCHEN: A COLLECTION OF HEALTHY SOUTHERN RECIPES

3 BRILLANT BREADS

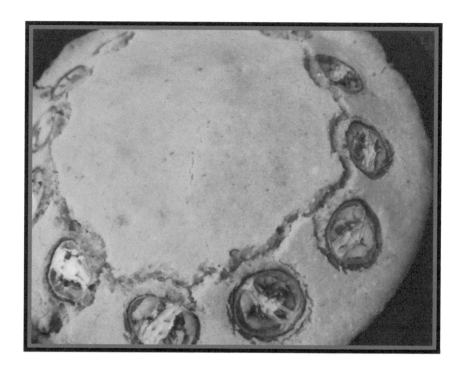

HOT JALAPENO HABANERO CORNBREAD

Ingredients:

1 ¼ cups organic cornmeal
¾ cup organic, unbleached, gluten-free, all-purpose flour
1 cup + 2 tbsp. rice or soy milk
1/3 cup vegetable oil
¼ cup water
¼ cup applesauce or 1 egg replacer
¼ cup vegan cane sugar
1 tbsp. + 1 tsp. melted vegan butter
1 tbsp. baking powder
½ tsp. baking soda
½ tsp. sea salt
1 jalapeno pepper, sliced
1 jalapeno, seeded and diced
2 scotch bonnet peppers, seeded and diced
¼ cup vegan shredded cheddar cheese (optional)

Instructions:

Preheat oven to 375 degrees Fahrenheit.

Grease a glass baking dish (4.5" x 8.5") or a cast iron skillet (9.5") with 1 tsp. butter and set aside.

In a bowl, combine all dry ingredients (cornmeal, flour, sugar, baking powder, baking soda, and salt). Mix in milk, oil, 1 tbsp. butter, and egg substitute. Stir by hand, but do not over mix the batter. Fold the peppers and cheese (optional) into the corn bread batter.

Pour the batter into the dish or skillet. Bake in the middle of the oven for 30 to 40 minutes. Use a toothpick to test the doneness, then slice, serve and enjoy!

YIELD: 12 pieces

BODACIOUS BUTTERMILK BISCUITS

Ingredients:

2 cups organic all-purpose flour + more to flour surface
1 cup vegan butter, chilled
1 cup organic soy milk
½ cup organic brown rice flour
2 tbsp. organic lard, chilled and cubed
1 tbsp. vegan butter, melted
1 tbsp. apple cider vinegar
1 tbsp. organic cane sugar
1 tbsp. aluminum-free baking powder
1 tsp fine sea salt
½ tsp baking soda

Instructions:

Preheat oven to 425 degrees Fahrenheit.

Use some of the melted butter to brush the bottom of a glass baking dish.

To make the buttermilk, add the apple cider vinegar to the soy milk, stir together, and set aside.

Mix all dry ingredients together in a large bowl. Add in chilled and cubed butter and lard. Blend together until the flour mixture has a crumbly texture. Make a well in the middle of the flour mixture. Pour the buttermilk into the well. Gradually add the flour into the milk until everything is incorporated. Feel free to use your hand to press the miscellaneous flour flakes in the bottom of the bowl into the dough ball.

Lightly flour a clean surface. Remove the dough ball from the large bowl and place it on the surface. Lightly flour the top of the ball as well as the rolling pin. Gently roll the dough 4 to 5 times. Fold the dough over twice and roll in out again. Repeat this step 3 more times. On the final fold, roll the dough out until its approximately ¼ inch in height.

Use a mold approximately 3" in diameter, or the rim of a drinking glass or coffee mug, to cut out 8 biscuits. Gently transfer the biscuits to the buttered dish and lightly brush the top of the biscuits with the remaining melted butter.

Bake the biscuits in the oven for 18 – 20 minutes. When they're done, the middle of the biscuits will have layers of flakes and the top will be golden brown.

Serve fresh out of the oven with syrup, jam, or your favorite food.

YIELD: 8 large biscuits

FROM THE CATWALK TO THE KITCHEN

DELECTABLE DINNER ROLLS

Ingredients:

3 ¼ cups organic bread flour or 3 ¼ cups organic all-purpose flour + 3 ¼ tsp baking powder
1 pack (approximately 2 ¼ tsp) quick rise active dry yeast
1 egg replacer
½ cup warm rice milk
½ cup warm water
¼ cup vegan butter + 1 ½ tsp. for brushing
2 tbsp. organic cane sugar
1 tsp. fine sea salt
½ tsp. organic liquid smoke

Preheat oven to 375 degrees Fahrenheit

Instructions:

Combine yeast, milk, water, and 1 tsp of sugar in a small bowl. Stir and set aside for 10 min, or until slightly foamy.

Sift dry ingredients together into a mixing bowl. Attach the dough hooks and turn the mixer on low. Pour the yeast liquid into the mixer bowl, then add the dry ingredients and mix for 10 seconds. Leaving the mixer on, add ¼ cup butter, egg replacer, and liquid smoke. Mix all ingredients together for 6-7 minutes while gradually increasing the speed from low to high.

Use ½ tsp of butter to brush the inside of a bowl. Remove the dough from the mixing bowl, form into a ball using your hands, and place the dough ball in the buttered bowl. Cover the bowl with a clean towel and set aside for 45 minutes to allow the dough to rise.

Brush ½ tsp butter into a round, glass baking dish and set aside. Transfer the dough onto a clean, lightly floured surface. Knead it for about a minute, then cut it into 10 pieces. Roll each piece of dough into a ball and symmetrically place each ball in the butter dish. Cover the dish with the towel and set aside for 30 minutes so the dough can rise again. The balls will expand to fill the dish. Bake in the middle of the oven for 18 minutes. Remove from over, brush the hot rolls with the remaining ½ tsp butter.

Yield: 12 rolls

SASSY SWEET POTATO CORNBREAD MUFFINS

Ingredients:

1 ½ cup organic yellow cornmeal
1 cup organic all-purpose flour
3 eggs, lightly beaten
½ cup organic cane sugar
½ cup melted vegan butter
¾ cup rice milk
½ cup baked sweet potato
2 tbsp. maple syrup
1 tbsp. baking powder
1 tsp. fine sea salt
½ tsp. baking soda
¼ tsp. ground cinnamon
¼ tsp. ground nutmeg

Instructions:

Preheat oven to 425 degrees Fahrenheit

Lightly oil or use muffin paper to line a muffin pan. Set aside.

Mix all of the dry ingredients, except the sugar, together in a large bowl and set aside.

Whip the butter and sugar together in a separate bowl. Add the eggs and give it a couple of stirs to semi-incorporate the eggs into the butter-sugar mixture. Set aside.

Using a food processor, whip the potato, milk, and syrup together until well blended. Add this potato mixture into the bowl with the butter-sugar-egg mixture. Use a blender to mix all of the ingredients together.

Scoop this mixture into the dry ingredients bowl. Use a blender to mix everything together and to make sure there are no lumps in the batter. Pour the finished batter into the muffin cups, filling each one approximately 80% full. Bake the muffins in the middle of the oven for 15-17 minutes (or until they pass the toothpick test).

Yield: 12 muffins

4 VIVACIOUS VEGETABLES

COUTURE COLLARD GREENS

Ingredients:

1 large bunch collard green leaves, cut into thin ribbons (approx. 8 cups)
1 medium shallot, finely chopped (approx. 1/3 cup)
1 jalapeno, finely chopped (approx. ¼ cup)
5 – 6 cloves roasted garlic cloves
1 cup warm water
1 cup low-sodium vegetable broth
2 tbsp. olive oil, divided
1 tbsp. tamarind chutney
1 tbsp. hickory smoked sea salt
1 tsp. raw sugar
1 tsp. sea salt
1 tsp. black pepper
½ tsp. smoked paprika
1 roasted red bell pepper, peeled and diced
1 pinch crushed red pepper flakes

Instructions:

Clean, de-rib, roll, and cut green leaves into thin ribbons.

Smash together the red pepper, garlic, oil, chutney, and red pepper flakes in a small bowl and set aside.

Heat a wok over medium high heat. Add remaining oil to the wok. Add the jalapenos and shallots, sauté for 1 minute. Then add the smashed mixture and continue to sauté for another minute or two.

Add the greens, stirring constantly to coat the greens with all other ingredients and to avoid sticking. Continue to lightly "fry" the greens for approximately 3 minutes.

Add all of the remaining ingredients. Cover the wok and allow the greens to come to a boil. Cook for 15 minutes.

Reduce the heat to medium low. Add more broth, if needed. Let the greens cook for another 25 minutes, or until tender. Serve and enjoy!

Servings: 4 - 6

GORGEOUS GREEN BEANS

Ingredients:

1 15 oz. bag of trimmed green beans
3 cloves garlic, thinly sliced
½ red bell pepper, thinly sliced
½ yellow bell pepper, thinly sliced
½ tbsp. olive oil
1 tsp. coarse sea salt
1/8 tsp. course black pepper

Instructions:

Preheat oven to 425 degrees Fahrenheit.

Place the green beans, peppers, and garlic on a flat, parchment-lined, baking dish. Then add the oil, salt, and pepper. Toss everything to evenly coat and season the vegetables.

Spread the vegetables out in the baking pan so they aren't stacked up on top of one another.

Place the pan on the top rack of the oven and roast the vegetables for 20 minutes.

Serve immediately.

Servings: 4 - 5

SMOKIN' SMOTHERED CABBAGE

Ingredients:

½ medium-size head of cabbage, thinly sliced
½ green bell pepper, cut into 1/4" diced pieces
½ white onion, ½" diced pieces
½ cup filtered water
1 tbsp. celery seeds or caraway seeds
½ tbsp. fine sea salt
2 tsp. vegan butter
1 tsp. olive oil
1 tsp. smoked sea salt
¼ tsp. ground black pepper
¼ tsp. ground white pepper

Instructions:

Add the onions, peppers, and oil to a pan over medium high heat. Cook for approximately 2 minutes, stirring regularly. Then add the cabbage, stir, and cook for 3 minutes.

Add all of the remaining ingredients to the pan. Stir to mix everything together. Reduce the heat to medium and cook for 15 minutes, stirring occasionally.

Serve and enjoy!

Servings: 5   6

RAVISHING ROASTED OKRA

Ingredients:

1 12 oz. pack whole fresh okra pods
1 tbsp. olive oil
1 tsp. sea salt
¼ tsp. ground black pepper

Instructions:

Preheat oven to 425 degrees Fahrenheit.

Line a flat baking dish with parchment paper and set aside.

Cut the large okra pods in half lengthwise and leave the smaller pods whole. Place them in a large bowl. Add all of the other ingredients and gently toss. Use your fingers to gently massage the oil and seasoning into each piece of okra.

Place the okra on the baking dish. Gently move the okra to flat them out. Try not to have the pieces of okra stacked on top of one another.

Roast the okra on the top rack of the oven for 15 minutes, then shake the baking dish (feel free to flip some of the okra pieces over). Return the pan to the oven and roast for 10 – 15 more minutes.

Serve and enjoy!

Servings: 4

5 MODISH MEATS

SLAMMIN' BBQ SALMON

Ingredients:

4 salmon steaks (as pictured), or fillets
1 tbsp. Old Bay seasoning
½ tbsp. garlic granules
¼ tsp. ground black pepper
Olive oil for brushing

(For the Sauce)
2 cups organic ketchup
½ cup finely diced white onion
½ cup spicy brown mustard
¼ cup organic Worcestershire sauce
¼ cup apple cider vinegar
2 tbsp. fresh lemon juice
½ tbsp. vegan butter
1 tsp. organic light brown sugar
1 tsp. garlic powder
¼ tsp. cayenne pepper
¼ tsp. ground black pepper

Instructions:

Preheat oven to 400 degrees Fahrenheit.

Line a flat baking dish with parchment paper and set aside.

To make the barbeque sauce: Add the onions and butter to a pot over medium high heat. Cook the onions until translucent, approximately 2 minutes.

Reduce to heat to medium low. Add all of the remaining ingredients into the pot. Stir to mix everything together. Allow the sauce to simmer for 3 minutes, stirring regularly to prevent sticking.

Cover the pot with a lid and reduce the heat to low. Let the sauce cook continue to simmer for 10 more minutes. Turn the heat off and allow the sauce to cool.

To cook the salmon: Make sure the fish is completely dry. Lightly brush each piece of salmon with the oil on both sides. Then season it on both sides (if cooking steaks), or on the meat side (if cooking fillets), and place them in the baking dish (skin side down if cooking fillets). Bake the salmon on the middle rack of the oven for 12 minutes.

Remove the salmon from the oven and brush it on both sides (if cooking steaks), or on the meat side (if cooking fillets) with some of the barbeque sauce. Use as much or as little sauce as you like. Store the remainder of the sauce in an air-tight jar or container in the refrigerator.

Return the salmon to the oven and continue to bake for 3 minutes.

Serve immediately and enjoy!

Servings: 4

BOLD BROASTED CHICKEN WINGS

Ingredients:

15 whole chicken wings
1 tbsp. Lawry's chicken & poultry rub
1 tbsp. salt-free mesquite seasoning
½ tbsp. Lawry's seasoning salt
½ tbsp. black pepper
Olive oil for brushing (approx. 2 tbsp.)

Instructions:

Preheat the oven to 425 degrees Fahrenheit

Combine all of the spices and seasonings in a small bowl. Stir to mix well and set aside.

Lightly coat a roasting rack with olive oil and set aside.

Make sure the chicken is completely dry. Fold the wings so the tip/flapper is securely tucked under the drumette. Lightly brush each wing with the oil.

Generously season each wing with the spice mix. Lay the wings on the prepare roasting rack, evenly spaced. Three rows with 5 wings in each row should suffice.

Roast the chicken on the top rack of the oven for 40 minutes.

Serve and enjoy!

Servings: 5

OUTRAGEOUS OVEN FRIED CATFISH

Ingredients:

4 fillets of catfish
1 cup organic soy milk
½ cup organic cornmeal
¼ cup panko breadcrumbs
1 tbsp. lemon juice
½ tbsp. organic flour
½ tsp. seasoning salt
½ tsp. garlic granules
½ tsp. seasoned pepper
½ tsp. ground paprika + more for dusting
½ tsp. dried oregano
¼ tsp. ground white pepper
A pinch of cayenne pepper (optional)
Olive oil spray (for coating)

Instructions:

Preheat oven to 400 degrees Fahrenheit

Line a flat baking dish with parchment paper and set aside.

Add the lemon juice to the cup of milk (to make buttermilk) and let it sit for 10 minutes.

Add the fish to a bowl, pour the buttermilk on top, cover the bowl, and allow the fish to marinate in the milk for 1 hour in the refrigerator.

Mix all of the remaining ingredients in a bowl. Stir to mix well. Spread the flour spice mix out onto a plate. Remove the fish from the milk marinade, shaking off any excess, and lay the fillet on top of the flour spice mix on the plate. Gently press the fish into the mixture. Repeat on the other side. Make sure each fillet is generously and well coated.

Lightly spray the top of the fish with olive oil, then lightly sprinkle on the paprika.

Lay each catfish fillet on the lined baking dish. Place on the top rack of the oven and bake for 45 minutes for thicker fillets and 35 minutes for thinner fillets.

Serve immediately.

Servings: 4

LOVELY LEMON HERBED CHICKEN

Ingredients:

1 whole chicken, cleaned, washed, and dried (approx. 4 lbs.)
1 lemon
1 small white onion, diced
3 springs of fresh rosemary, cut into thirds
6 - 10 cloves of garlic
1 tbsp. melted vegan butter
1 tbsp. grapeseed oil
1 tbsp. onion granules
1 tbsp. garlic granules
1 tbsp. Lawry's seasoning salt
1 tbsp. Lawry's chicken & poultry rub
1 tbsp. ground sweet paprika
½ tbsp. ground black pepper

Instructions:

Preheat the oven to 425 degrees Fahrenheit.

Place the chicken in a roasted pan. Mix the butter and oil together and brush it all over the chicken, inside and outside.

Add the last six ingredients in a small bowl. Stir to mix well. Evenly coat the outside of the chicken with spice mix. Season the inside of the chicken with what's left after seasoning the outside.

In a large bowl, add the lemon, garlic, onions, and rosemary. Toss together well and stuff into the chicken's cavity. If all of it doesn't fit inside, place the remainder of the mix around the chicken in the pan.

Cover the pan and bake on the middle rack of the oven for 75 - 90 minutes. Let it rest for 10-15 minutes before cutting into it.

Servings: 8

6 SEDUCTIVE SIDES

LUMINOUS LIMA BEANS

Ingredients:

16 oz. of fresh or frozen beans
½ tbsp. olive oil
½ tbsp. vegan butter
1 cup low-sodium vegetable broth
3/4 cups filtered water
½ tbsp. hickory smoked sea salt
½ tbsp. garlic granules
½ tsp. onion powder
¼ tsp. sea salt
¼ tsp. black pepper

Instructions:

In a medium-sized saucepan on medium high heat, sauté the garlic and the hickory smoked sea salt for 1 minute. Smash the garlic and the sea salt into the oil as the oil gets hot.

Add the lima beans and onion powder to the pot. Then stir the mixture for another minute. Once the peas are well coated with the oil/salt mixture, and all of the remaining ingredients. Let the seasoned beans cook uncovered for 3 minutes. Then cover the saucepan and reduce the heat to medium. Let the beans cook for 35 minutes.

To test for doneness, hold a bean between your thumb and index finger. If it smashes easily it's done. If it's still a little hard, allow the beans to continue to cook for another 10 – 15 minutes on medium heat.

Servings: 6

MARVELOUS MAC N' CHEESE

Ingredients:

12 oz. pkg. organic (gluten-free) brown rice macaroni pasta
10 oz. shredded vegan cheddar cheese
7 oz. shredded vegan jack cheese
4 oz. shredded vegan mozzarella cheese
2 ½ cups rice milk
½ cup panko bread crumbs (natural, gluten free)
¼ tsp. sea salt
1/8 tsp. ground nutmeg
1/8 tsp. white pepper
Butter to coat the baking dish
Paprika for dusting

Preheat oven to 375 degrees Fahrenheit

Instructions:

Butter a baking dish and set aside. Cook the macaroni al dente (according to the package directions) and set aside.

Heat 1 ½ cup rice milk in a medium size sauce pan over medium heat. Add cheddar cheese and whisk until melted. Add jack cheese and whisk until melted. Add mozzarella cheese and whisk until melted.

Add the seasonings (salt, pepper, nutmeg) once all the cheeses have melted together into a smooth, creamy cheese sauce. Stir to mix well.

Pour the cheese sauce over the cooked macaroni. Add the remaining milk, approximately 1 cup, and gently stir to mix together. Pour the macaroni and cheese into the buttered dish.

Sprinkle the bread crumbs over the mixture to cover the entire dish. Top the bread crumbs with a light dusting of paprika. Bake until the cheese is bubbling around the edges and the top is lightly browned, approximately 20 minutes. Allow to cool slightly, then serve.

Servings: 8 - 10

BRASSY BLACK EYED PEAS

Ingredients:

16 oz. of fresh or frozen peas
3 – 4 roasted garlic cloves
2 cups water
2 cups vegetable broth
1 tbsp. olive oil or vegan butter
½ tsp. smoked sea salt
½ tsp. onion powder
¼ tsp. sea salt
¼ tsp. black pepper

Instructions:

In a medium-sized saucepan on medium high heat, sauté oil or butter, garlic, and smoked sea salt for 1 minute. Smash the garlic and the smoked sea salt into the oil as the oil gets hot.

Add black eyed peas and onion powder. Then stir the mixture for another minute. Once the peas are well coated with the oil and the seasonings, add the remaining ingredients. Let the mixture boil uncovered for 3 minutes.

Cover the saucepan and reduce the heat to medium. Let the peas cook for 35 – 40 minutes.

To test for doneness, hold a pea between your thumb and index finger. If it smashes easily it's done. If it's still a little hard, allow the peas to continue to cook for another 10 – 15 minutes on medium heat.

Serve and enjoy!

Servings: 6

PRETTY POTATO SALAD

Ingredients:

2 medium-sized white potatoes, peeled and diced small
2 eggs + 1 for garnish
2 tbsp. pickled relish
1/3 cup + 1 tbsp. vegan mayo
1 tbsp. Dijon mustard
1 tbsp. red onion, diced small + 4 thin rings for garnish
¼ tsp. sea salt
¼ tsp. ground black pepper
¼ tsp. celery seed or fresh chopped dill
Sprinkle of ground paprika for garnish

Instructions:

Add potatoes and eggs to a pot with water at least 1" above the contents. Cook covered over medium-high heat until the potatoes are tender. Remove pot from the heat. Using a slotted spoon, transfer the potatoes from the pot to a medium-sized bowl (make sure no water is transferred to the bowl with the potatoes).

Recover the pot and return to the stove top. Allow the eggs to continue cooking in the heated water only, no heat required. Add all remaining ingredients, except for the eggs, paprika, and onions rings to the bowl with the potatoes. Gently stir to mix everything together. Set aside.

Pour all of the water out of the pot and set it in the sink. Run cold water into the pot from the facet. Peel the eggs under low pressure running cold water. Set one egg aside. Dice the remaining two eggs into small cubes (similar in size to the potatoes) and add to the salad. Fold the eggs in to incorporate them into the rest of the ingredients.

Pour the potato salad into a serving bowl. Cut the remaining egg into 4 wedges and place them, along with the onion rings, on top of the salad. Sprinkle with top with paprika, then chill for at least 2 hours in the refrigerator (optional), and serve.

Servings: 4

7 DAZZLING DESSERTS

SEXY SWEET POTATO PIE

Ingredients:

3 medium Garnet Jewel sweet potatoes
2 egg whites, slightly whipped
1 whole egg, lightly beaten
1 prepared pie crust
½ cup almond, cashew, and hazelnut milk (or any non-dairy milk)
½ cup of light brown sugar
¼ cup of organic cane sugar
2 tbsp. melted vegan butter
2 tbsp. vanilla extract
2 tsp. cinnamon
2 tsp. nutmeg
2 tsp. ginger
1 tsp. salt
½ tsp almond extract
½ tsp. orange extract
½ tsp. ground cloves
½ tsp. allspice
½ tsp. fine sea salt

Instructions:

Preheat the oven to 375 degrees Fahrenheit.

Add the potatoes to a pan filled with water. Make sure the water covers at least 70% of the potatoes. Boil over medium high heat until the potatoes are softened completely, for approximately 15 minutes (depending on the size of the potatoes). Remove the potatoes from the pot and set aside to semi-cool.

Pour the remaining water out of the pot. Peel the potatoes and add them back into the pot. Mash the potatoes well, until there are no lumps, and set aside.

In a large bowl, cream the butter and sugar together. Add the eggs, the milk, and stir well. Then add the rest of the ingredients and mix well. Pour the mixture in the bowl into the pot with the potatoes. Stir to mix well. Use an electric beater if needed.

Continue to mix until all of the lumps are removed.

Pour the filling into the pie shell. Bake the sweet potato pie on the middle rack in the oven for 45 minutes to an hour.

Remove the pie from the oven and allow it to cool to room temperature. Cut and serve.

Yield: 8 slices

HIBISCUS ROSE RED VELVET CUPCAKES

Ingredients:

(For Cupcakes)
1 ¼ cups organic all-purpose flour
1 cup organic cane sugar
¾ cup organic almond milk
¼ cup minus 2 tbsp. organic almond milk
1/3 cup sunflower seed or safflower oil
2 tbsp. organic cocoa powder
1 - 2 tbsp. dried hibiscus petals
1 tbsp. rose water
2 tsp. vanilla extract
1 tsp. Apple Cider Vinegar
1/2 tsp. non-aluminum baking powder
1/2 tsp. baking soda
1/2 tsp. kosher or fine sea salt
1/4 tsp. almond extract
1 bottle of vegan red food coloring

(For Frosting)
1 cup organic confectioners' sugar
8 oz. vegan cream cheese, softened
2 tbsp. vegan butter, softened
1 tsp. vanilla extract

Instructions:

Preheat the oven at 350F for 15 minutes.

Line a 12 cup muffin tin with liners (paper, silicone, etc). In a medium size bowl, mix together ¾ cup milk and vinegar. Set aside to curdle (this will take about 5 minutes). Then stir in the oil, food coloring, and extracts. Whisk it thoroughly to combine all of these ingredients together.

Slightly heat the remaining milk and steep with the hibiscus, then strain the flavored milk and add the rose water. Set aside.

Sift together the flour, cocoa powder, baking powder, baking soda, and salt in a large bowl. Then stir in the sugar. Make a well in the dry ingredients, then slowly add the wet mixtures of milk. Stir the batter until all the ingredients come together. Small lumps are okay. Take care to see that you do not over mix; otherwise you will not get fabulously fluffy cupcakes.

Fill each muffin tin 75% full of the batter. Place the muffin tin in the oven and bake for approx. 16 - 20 minutes, or until a toothpick inserted in the middle of the cupcake comes out clean or with very little crumbs. Transfer the pan to a wire rack and let it remain there for 5 minutes. Then carefully remove the cupcakes from the pan and let them cool completely before frosting.

For the frosting, mix all ingredients together in a bowl until smooth. Set the bowl in the refrigerator for at least 30 minutes. Gently spread the frosting on top of each cupcakes, serve, and enjoy!

Yield: 12 cupcakes

LUSCIOUS LEMON POUND CAKE

Ingredients:

(For the Cake)
3 cups minus 6 tbsp. unbleached organic all-purpose flour
    + more for dusting
6 tbsp. organic corn starch
6 organic eggs, room temperature
½ large lemon, zested (approx. 1 tsp.)and juiced (approx. 1 tbsp.)
3 cups organic cane sugar
2 cups vegan butter
½ cup almond milk
2 tsp. kosher salt
2 tsp. vanilla extract
1 tsp. lemon extract

(For the Glaze)
½ cup organic powdered sugar
1 large lemon, juiced (approx.. 2 tbsp.)
1 large lemon, zested (approx. 1 tsp.)

Instructions:

Preheat oven to 350 degrees Fahrenheit.

Grease and lightly dust the inside of a Bundt cake pan with flour. Set aside.

In bowl #1, mix together the milk, juice, extract, and zest. Stir and set aside.

In bow #2, add all dry ingredients. Stir to mix together. Run the flour mix through a sifter 6 times. (Congratulations, you've just made cake flour!)

In bowl #3, using a mixer, cream together the butter and sugar until creamy. Add the eggs individually (add one egg and mix to incorporate, then add another egg, repeat) and mix until well incorporated.

Add the ingredients from bowls #1 and #3 into bowl #2, alternating half of each mix, starting with the dry ingredient mix. Blend the ingredients after each addition. After all ingredients have been added into bowl #2, continue to mix to ensure everything is mixed together well.

Pour the batter evenly into the cake pan. Bake on the middle rack of the oven for 60 - 70 minutes. Use a skewer to test for doneness. Allow the cake to cool completely.

To make the glaze, whisk all ingredients together in a bowl until smooth. Carefully remove the cake from the pan and invert it onto a plate or cake stand. Pour the glaze evenly over the cake, and then sprinkle the top of the cake with the zest.

Servings: 12 – 14 slices

BANGIN' BANANA PUDDING

Ingredients:

2 ½ cups non-dairy milk (preferably a blend of coconut, almond, and chia), divided
1/3 cup all-purpose flour
¼ cup organic cane sugar
¼ cup organic powdered sugar
6 bananas
2 large egg yolks or egg replacer
1 13.5 fl. oz. can full-fat coconut milk, chilled 8 hours or overnight
1 5.4 fl. oz. can organic coconut cream
1 tbsp. organic cornstarch
1 tbsp. vanilla extract
1 ½ tsp. fresh lemon juice
1 tsp. cold water
Vanilla wafers (preferably Madagascar vanilla)
A dash of sea salt

Instructions:

Preheat oven to 375 degrees Fahrenheit.

Cut four bananas into half inch pieces. Toss them in a bowl with lemon juice, and then spread them out on a flat, parchment lined baking dish. Bake the bananas on the top rack of the oven for 15 minutes. Remove and set aside to cool.

Once cooled, place the baked banana pieces into a food processor along with ½ cup of milk and vanilla extract. Blend until smooth and set aside.

Add the flour, cane sugar, and salt to a pot over medium heat. Gradually add the remaining milk, and stir to mix the ingredients together. Add the egg yolks, one at a time, stirring in between each one. Continue to cook the mixture for another 8-10 minutes, stirring frequently to avoid sticking.

Add the pureed bananas to the pot. Whisk vigorously to blend all ingredients together. The pudding should be smooth ... no lumps allowed.

In a separate bowl, add the cornstarch and water. Stir to mix, and then add the cornstarch slurry into a pot. Stir to mix well. Continue to cook for 5 minutes, stirring frequently to prevent sticking. Turn the heat off once the mixture starts to thicken.

Using an electric mixer, whip the coconut cream on high speed until fluffy (approximately 5-7 minutes). Then fold the whipped coconut cream into the pureed banana pudding.

Cut the remaining two bananas into bite-size pieces and place them in the bottom of a glass dessert dish. Line the inside of the dish with the vanilla wafers. Then gently pour (or spoon in) the banana pudding on top of the cut bananas while keeping the wafers securely in place.

Drain the excess liquid from the can of chilled coconut milk. Spoon out the solidified coconut milk from the can into a bowl. Whisk it on high speed until smooth, approximately 20 seconds. Then add the powdered sugar, and whisk again for another 20 seconds. Be sure to start the mixer out on low and gradually move up to high speed. Do not overmix! The coconut milk should be light and fluffy.

Spoon the coconut whipped cream onto the middle of the banana pudding. Garnish the top of the pudding with more vanilla wafers and refrigerate for at least 4 hours before serving.

Servings: 10 - 12

8 UNTIL NEXT TIME

This cookbook took what seemed like forever to complete and publish. During the 6 year process, I had many people asked me about the book's progress. Everyone from family, friends, culinary students and associates inquired about my endeavor. I started developing and tweaking these recipes while working in corporate America.

Just like the process of establishing my culinary foundation, my evolution of becoming a cookbook author has been a uniquely interesting journey. Throughout my years of working in corporate America, traveling the world, and volunteering for a non-profit organization (where I eventually becoming the lead Culinary Educator for the entire foundation), I continued to develop and perfect my cookbook recipes.

No matter where life took me, I never stopped cooking. I continued to conceive and capture my culinary creations; although there were times I was so overtaken with creativity that I forget to document my culinary process (SMH). The outcome? I have a multitude of delicious and healthy-ish recipes to share with you.

So, I hope you enjoy my re-vamped family recipes in this cookbook, and be on the lookout for more cookbooks from me. Culinary Kisses presents ... to be continued.

Until then, "whatever you cook, cook with love!"

Food n' Kisses,
Chef Angela-Michelle

9 WHERE TO FIND US

Website: www.CulinaryKisses.com

Blog: www.CulinaryKisses.com/blog

Newsletter: http://eepurl.com/uaaGr

@CulinaryKisses

Facebook | Twitter | Instagram

You Tube | Tik Tok

10 ABOUT THE AUTHOR

Chef Angela-Michelle is a culinary diva! She takes what she learned from her family growing up and mixes it with the knowledge she gained from her culinary travels. Then she adds a smidgen of flair from the fashion and modeling industry and stirs it all up to create a uniquely delicious dish. She might even wear 3" stilettos and a LBD (little black dress) while doing it, all while making it look flawless and effortless. Angela is definitely a triple threat in her own right.

Visit www.CulinaryKisses.com to learn more about Angela's company and what they do. They offer several services including:

Hands-on Cooking Classes
Live Virtual Interactive Cooking Classes
On-line Culinary Classes
Themed Cooking Parties
Private Cooking Lessons
Live Cooking Demonstrations
Corporate Wellness Programs

Feel free to email the author directly at Angela@CulinaryKisses.com.

#CULINARYKISSES
#CHEFANGELAMICHELLE
#FOODANDKISSES

CPSIA information can be obtained
at www.ICGtesting.com
Printed in the USA
LVHW071531210620
658638LV00001B/4